HEAVENLY DISCIPLESHIP

STUDY GUIDE

HANNAH MORRELL

Abiding Life Press

©2014 by Hannah Morrell

Published by Abiding Life Press
A division of Abiding Life Ministries International
P.O. Box 620998, Littleton, CO 80162

Printed in the United States of America

All rights reserved. No part of this publication may be reproduced, stored in
a retrieval system, or transmitted in any form or by any means—electronic,
mechanical, photocopy, recording, or any other—without the prior written
permission of the publisher. The only exception is brief quotations in
printed reviews.

For Mike, who walked with Jesus
and continues to do so.

Contents

Chapter 1 Heavenly Discipleship 1
   Worldly vs. Heavenly 1

Chapter 2 The Disciple and Self 4
   Is Life Futile? 4
   Get a Life! 5
   Christ is your life! 7
   He is the Way! 9
   No Joy in Life 11

Chapter 3 What Suits the Heavenly Disciple? 16
   Indifference 17
   Fear 18
   Procrastination 20
   Bitterness 22
   Pessimism 23
   Inadequacy 24
   One Goal 24
   Sex 25
   Judgment 27
   Humility 28
   Addictions 28
   Anxiety 29
   Justification 31

Chapter 4 The Disciple and God 32
   Ministering to Desire 34
   Pushed God Too Far? 35
   A Wiped Memory! 36
   The Disciple and Failure 36
   The Disciple and the Law of Liberty 38
   Remember, It's a Relationship 40
   The Divine Escalator 40
   Stressed by God 41
   There Is No God in the Past 41
   Prayer 42
   The Hurting Father 42
   God is Love 43

His Perfect Will 43
What Is Not the Will of God 45
Learning Obedience...46
Hearing God 47
Pride 48
He Makes Your World Beautiful................................49

Chapter 5   The Disciple and Faith.....................................50
Faith Introduction..50
The Disciple Needs Faith 52
Why Do You Not Believe?..53
Jesus Is Faith...54
Exercising Faith...54
Bring Faith to the Table 55
Faith and Repentance 56
Faith Is Finding...56
Faith Is Being Honest with God...............................57
Faith and Others..57
Faith and Waiting 58
Faith and the Glory of God..59
Faith Is Upsetting...59
The Faith Theft...61
Faith Trusts God for the Family................................61
Faith Lets God Carry the Burdens 62
Faith Is Not Immediate Results................................62
Faith and Problems..63
Faith and Simplicity...65
The Faith Cycle...66
Faith Counts 67
Satan 67

Chapter 6   Discipleship Basics...69
Discipling on the Fringe 70
Beginning at the End! 71
The Disciple and Sin 72
Avoiding Self-righteousness
and Unrighteousness 73
The Disciple and Intelligence....................................73
The Blown-up Bridge...74
The Law 75
The Disciple and Individuality...................................79

The Disciple and Miracles 80
The Disciple and a Normal Conversion 83
The Disciple and Vocation 83
Bad Luck 84
The Division of Soul and Spirit 85
Weary of the Do-Do's 86
Give to No Man/Give to Every Man! 87
Self-Hatred 87
Obsessions 89
He Is Everywhere 90
With Him or in Him 90
Independence 90
Comfortable with Honesty 91
Satisfaction 92
Total Commitment 93
Spiritual Bullies 95
Remember the Basics 96
Moving On 97

Chapter 7   The Disciple and Suffering 98

Chapter 8   The Disciple and the Word 102
No Answer in Scripture 102
Printing Press 104
The Word Became Flesh 105
Life Witnesses to Jesus 105

Chapter 9   The Disciple and Others 106
Witnessing The Absolute Truth 106
Bless Those Who Curse You 108
Invisible Strings 108
Ministering With or Ministering To 109
Faithful Are the Wounds of a Friend 110
When the Disciple Is the Enemy 110
Standing Alone 111
Without Conscience 112
Verbal Beatings 115
Get off the Throne 115
Others Need to Change? 116

Chapter 10 The Disciple and Ending Well 118

Chapter I
Heavenly Discipleship

The Church often specializes in worldly discipleship and emphasizes so many of the wrong things. The people at the top of the totem pole dictate to the people at the bottom what must be done to become spiritual giants, and they build bigger and bigger kingdoms composed of those who too often end up worshipping the person instead of God. Mike used to say that if unbelievers could accomplish what was set forth as discipleship, then it was not Christian, and therefore its goal was not discovering the expansion of Christ's Life within. Relying on a formula for discipleship enables an unbeliever to do it, because there is nothing supernatural about it. Instead, Mike calls us to see the fruit instead of getting stuck at the peel.

Worldly vs. Heavenly

How have you experienced both worldly and heavenly discipleship? (p 1)

Can you think of times you have (or someone else has) allowed the knowledge of the Bible to take precedence over familiarity with its Author? (p 2)

Are you more likely to think of the steps you need to take to secure God than about how He has secured you? (p 2)

How have you employed worldly formulas to become spiritual? (p 2)

Can you see how you have walked in the flesh, living in the condition of pride? (p 3)

Do you believe your identity is based in God, or do you see areas in which you grasp what is earthly to build up your self? (p 3)

How have you bought into the pyramid scheme of worldly discipleship? (pp 3, 4)

Have you tried to climb the pyramid to get something you thought Christ had not given you? (pp 4, 5)

Do you understand how nothing can come of such comparing and competing based in the work of man, rather than in the work of God? (pp 4, 5)

How have you gotten stuck examining the peel while missing the fruit? (p 6)

Have you witnessed or been a part of the spiritual chess game, where professional Christians jockey for position? (p 6)

Father, I no longer want to work at this pyramid scheme, because I see the futility in it. It is not of You, and I am losing my life in the midst of it. Thank You that there is a better way, a way that gives life rather than taking it. I want to understand that in You I already have everything I need and there is nothing more to add.

Chapter 2
The Disciple and Self

Many of us wander through life believing that we will have no hope of a good experience with Jesus, when all the while we have received His Life within and have access to all that we need simply by looking to Him. No wonder we get a little burned out on life! The answer, though, lies not in trying to fix our current life, but through accepting His and watching Him bring joy to the situation that seemed impossible. It is a beautiful way to live, because it is not dependent on the circumstances around us. We must humble ourselves, though, and look to Jesus instead of continuing to search for every answer other than Him.

Is Life Futile?

Have you believed that life is futile and developed a vested interest in life's becoming ever more pointless? (pp 7, 8)

How has our culture promoted this idea that life is pointless? (pp 8, 9)

In what way can you commit to pursuing that which has value to your inner life and will expand eternally? (pp 9, 10)

Get a Life!

Has your experience been similar to what Mike describes as walking through the world as God's highest creation, defeated at every turn and then depleted? (p 11)

How was Jesus' life on the earth different from the one you walk on a daily basis? (p 12)

Do you believe that Christ's life within you can overcome everything the world throws at it? (pp 12, 13)

What difference does it make in your life to understand that you are one with Christ and part of a new race, the children of God? (p 13)

What is your response to Mike's calling you an oak rather than a weed becoming an oak? (p 13)

Do you see how the proof of what we are is revealed through our struggles rather than our victories? (p 14)

How have you experienced the awakening wherein you lay aside the flesh, not because you want to be holy, but because you recognize you have already been made the recipient of a holy life? (pp 14, 15)

Have you noticed the things that do not give you a lift in your spirit if you do them? What behaviors do not give you that lift? Do you see that they are not natural for Christ's life? (p 15)

What life experiences have given you lessons pointing to the fact that your life in Christ is The Way? (p 16)

Have you sensed incompleteness when Jesus is not the center of life? (p 17)

What things besides Jesus have you tried to satisfy the craving of your heart? (p 17)

Are you recognizing that anything outside of Jesus simply does not suit us as believers? (p 18)

Christ is Your Life!

Have you wondered whether or not you were truly saved? (p 18)

Do you believe that the greatness of your faith is not determined by how much you receive and experience, but rather by how long you can wait without receiving or experiencing anything? (p 18)

Do you feel frustration when you walk in the flesh? (p 19)

Are you ever filled with anxiety and realize it is because the dead you is not improving, helping, or assisting in the human experience? (p 19)

Are you ready to stop trying to improve, accept your death and burial, and turn for help only to Christ's life? (pp 19, 20)

Have you allowed your experience to hold greater significance than the truth of God? (pp 20, 21)

How have you confused the baggage of the old man with being the old man? (p 21)

Have you experienced a dip in your spirit as you set your mind on a lie, because it does not suit the new life you have within? (p 22)

Do you see that the baggage is God's stronghold to keep you near to Himself in dependence? (p 22)

Have you tried the simple exercise of refusing to yield when the world, body, and emotions stir the mind to go visit the baggage? Did it work? (p 22)

Have you experienced the struggle when you go to the flesh for satisfaction, since Christ is your true nature? (p 23)

Does the illustration of worshipping a rag doll as a picture of trusting the old man bring clarity? (p 23)

He is the Way!

What lesser truths have stolen your focus from the greatest truth? (pp 24, 25)

Have you experienced self's control over you as you made every attempt either to satisfy it or to avoid it? (p 25)

What questions in your life fade when you consider Jesus? (p 26)

Are you familiar with the happiness received from focusing on Jesus rather than on your problems or circumstances? (p 27)

Have you noticed that when Jesus is not considered to be the answer, questions immediately increase and you live in chaos? (pp 28, 29)

Does it make sense that there is so little advice on relationships in Scripture because the writers assumed we were doing the basics of keeping Christ in the center of life, making Him the answer, and simply abiding in Him? (pp 29, 30)

Have you found people with the mindset that since Jesus did not "work" for them, He will not for others? (p 30)

Do you agree that the self-life's desire to control causes most issues, problems, and questions? (p 30)

Have you met believers who are not any closer to the peace that Jesus gives even though they have spent much time looking for answers to their problems? (p 30)

Do you see that these answers for which they are looking are outside of Christ and there is peace only in Christ? (p 30)

Have you seen that presuming every man can have his own
truth leads to believing that ultimately there is no truth? (p 31)

Do you understand the difference between leading people to a
system versus absolute truth in Jesus? (p 32)

After accepting Truth (Jesus), have you found any lesser truths
that brought freedom? (p 33)

No Joy in Life

Have correct doctrine, church order, emotional experiences,
intellectual pursuits, methods, gimmicks, programs, self-
examination, self-centeredness, anger, frustration, or slander
brought about peace, joy, rest, or a perfect life? (p 34)

Do you want the perfect life as described in Matthew 5? (p 34)

Can you list a few notions you have observed of what is believed to compose the Christian life? Do you see how these cannot stand when compared to the acceptance and expression of Christ's life? (p 35)

Have you seen how the world advocates sin and self-centeredness as a means to satisfaction, but those never give what they promise? (pp 35, 36)

Do you understand how sin and punishment walk hand in hand, so there is no reason for condemnation from any other? (p 36)

How does this revelation affect how you allow yourself to live in self-condemnation or by judging others? (p 36)

Is man created by nature to sin? (pp 36, 37)

How have you witnessed the parasitical nature of sin? (p 37)

Can you believe that abundant Life is found in a person, not in words or actions? (p 38)

Do you see the advantage to those who keep Christianity complex is that they never have to get around to living it? (p 39)

How have you experienced worldly discipleship's attempts to prepare the believer with knowledge of what to do in every conceivable situation? (p 39)

If God wants you to walk in faith with an empty bag you trust Him to fill, how does this change how you go about your day? (p 40)

Can you identify times when you walked in true humility, emptied of self, and were filled with the fullness of Christ? (p 40)

List some ways you have seen demonstrated that everything giving a disciple joy comes from a relationship with Christ, the most natural way to live. (p 41)

Do you agree that the Bible is not needed to prove that Jesus is the true way, because truth proves itself? (p 42)

Have you tried to create a relationship instead of recognizing that you already have one? (pp 42, 43)

Father, thank You for allowing Jesus to dwell in me and for giving me access to this amazing Life I would never have known apart from Him. I want to experience the joy that He brings, not because I am working hard to achieve this joy, but rather because it is the natural outcome of living in relationship with You.

Chapter 3
What Suits the Heavenly Disciple?

As a heavenly disciple, we are not suited for some of the things that have controlled us in the past. Mike walks through discussions of several different idols and how they no longer make sense for us. Often I think we focus on what we should not be doing rather than simply realizing that those things no longer fit who we are. What a difference this makes in the anxiety level with which we approach our relationship with God!

What Suits the Heavenly Disciple?

Does obedience suit and benefit the believer? (p 45)

Have you decided you do not have to love or forgive someone in your life because this might encourage his bad behavior, or have you learned this is life-killing, since loving is for your sake rather than the other person's? (pp 45, 46)

Do you believe no person can make you miserable, but rather you choose to be miserable? How does this belief change how you live? (p 46)

Can you describe a time you had one problem turn to three when you refused to love your enemy? (p 47)

Do you see the difference between obedience in order to change what you are versus obedience to reveal what you are? (p 47)

How does the revelation that sin does not suit you make your life different? (pp 47, 48)

Can you think of ways you have discovered Jesus' commands feeding rather than imposing upon your life? (p 48)

Indifference

Have you struggled with indifference? (p 48)

Have you experienced times when Jesus took even the most mundane existence and filled it with expectation? (p 49)

In what ways are you not savoring life? Do you see it is because you have become your own heaven or hell, not embracing Jesus as the One who flavors life pleasantly? (p 49)

Are you willing to give yourself to something more precious and great than yourself, and thus truly rest? (p 50)

Fear

What has fear prompted you to do? (p 50)

Can you see that fear—the enemy of faith—is spawned when we lack dependence on God? (pp 50, 51)

How has it proven true in your life that the greater your inferiority, the greater your attempts to protect yourself and the greater your fears? (pp 51, 52)

What is the difference between living as a sparrow and living in fear? (p 52)

What is the root of your fear? (p 53)

Are you willing to invite fear out? (p 53)

Do you see the difference between confronting fear and changing direction to head back into the presence of God? (p 53)

Take a moment to pray as Mike led.

"Father, I am sorry that my focus has been fear. I have looked to myself to sustain myself, to control my world, to find security, and I have reaped the consequences. I am full of fear. I now invite fear out; I make You my focus. Let Your presence heal me. Amen."

In times of separation from loved ones or from familiar surroundings, are you willing to see how much God would have you learn in it, remembering you have a God rather than dwelling on your fear? (p 54)

Procrastination

Have you experienced indecision's being worse than a bad decision? (p 55)

Why do you procrastinate? (p 55)

Do you recognize and appreciate the process towards maturity in your own life? (p 55)

Do you see how the turmoil arising from decision-making is really a faith issue? (p 56)

How have you seen God structuring your life to ensure that you do not place your trust in something other than Him? (p 57)

Are you willing to say, "Father, this is my decision; I want Your will not mine," and then act? (p 57)

When have you acted as though your chooser is broken? (pp 57, 58)

Are you willing to trust and rest after refusing procrastination and choosing what seems good to you, while saying, "Your will be done"? (p 58)

Have you wrongly assumed that something fun cannot possibly be God's will? (p 58)

How have you treated God as though His presence is so small that His will has to be sought with a magnifying glass? (p 59)

Do you believe that your decisions are not weighty enough to destroy you? How does that belief change the way you live? (p 59)

Bitterness

How have you experienced an initial sense of satisfaction from obsession over an offense that in the end left you or someone else cheated, destroyed, physically sick, or even suicidal? (p 60)

Have you seen bitterness in your life spring from false accusations or being used? (p 61)

Are you willing to share your bitterness with Jesus and watch Him lift the oppression? (p 61)

Pessimism

Do you know a pessimistic person, or are you one yourself? (p 62)

Do you see how pessimism develops from self-centeredness? (p 62)

Is there someone in your life to whom you need to tell the truth in love? (p 63)

Does it make sense that doing for others allows the pessimist to find life? (p 63)

Inadequacy

Have you experienced feelings of inadequacy, deficiency, and wanting to withdraw? (p 64)

How would your life change if instead you approached life's challenges with excitement because of confidence? (p 64)

Do you see the difference between actually being inadequate and being fully adequate in Christ but still focused on shortcomings? (pp 64, 65)

Are you willing to own and confess your weakness, allowing Him to step in and change things? (p 65)

One Goal

Have you experienced yourself falling apart when an inward division arose? (p 65)

How have you been a divided believer, clinging to your idols while also trying to hold Christ? (pp 65, 66)

In discipleship, do you see how Jesus must be presented as something better so idols are dropped in favor of Him? (pp 66, 67)

Have you witnessed any benefit in self-centeredness? (p 67)

Do you agree that we are suited for selflessness and giving ourselves to something bigger than self? (pp 67, 68)

Sex

Have you experienced sex as a need for acceptance rather than a purely physical need? (p 68)

Have you tried to get from sex what it cannot give? (pp 68, 69)

As change in the estimation we have of ourselves can come only through exchange of our life for Christ's life, can you let go of trying to get this inner change from sex? (p 69)

How important is it to identify Christ's acceptance and worth as your own, so that sex is not as important as the welfare of the other person? (p 69)

Do you understand how feelings of rejection start affairs? (p 69)

Can you see the wisdom in not saying you will never have an affair, but saying you are not going to place yourself in the location where you have to find out? (p 70)

Have you tried not thinking about sex and by so doing spent every waking moment thinking about it? (p 70)

Does it make sense that attempting to kill natural attraction is error because you do not want to kill attraction for your mate? (p 70)

Have you seen unbelievers pursuing believers for the desirable anointing of Christ? (pp 70, 71)

Judgment

Have you experienced how judging moves you away from Jesus? (p 71)

How have you discovered that at the center of God's heart is a cross rather than judgment? (p 72)

Is it apparent we are suited for love and not judgment? (p 72)

Have you judged others and assigned God's glory to yourself? (p 73)

Do you agree judging is best left to God, since when we judge, we always judge wrongly? (pp 73, 74)

Is it helpful to see God's acceptance as based on birth rather than behavior, and thus we can set others and ourselves free from being judged? (p 74)

Humility

Have you humbly recognized you have nothing with which to compete, because you only have what Christ gives? (p 75)

Do you see why we only boast in God, because He alone gives us all the tools we need as He works out what He wants from our lives? (p 75)

Addictions

Is it obvious an addiction is a relationship built with a coping mechanism? (p 76)

What addictions have controlled your life? (pp 76, 77)

Have you found it to be true that addiction's one goal is to sacrifice your life? (p 77)

When an addiction seems it will overwhelm you, are you willing to bring your addiction before God, recognize the addiction is no friend, and draw near to God while living for the morning? (p 77)

Have you ever lost the enjoyment of an addiction before you officially "quit"? (p 78)

Anxiety

Is the source of your anxiety and fear your trusting a weak self, since you were not created to carry all the concerns of life? (p 79)

How does recognizing that you were created to be dependent change the way you live? (p 79)

What do you need to give Jesus to carry? (p 80)

Are you willing to cast anxiety on Jesus, taking your hands off and recognizing you have a God who can take care of it? (p 80)

To what places have you gone through His strength alone as you were freed from anxiety? What places could you go in the future as you experience this freedom? (p 80)

Do you agree that anxiety does not suit you? (p 81)

Justification

Have you listened to arguments of self-justification or given some yourself? (p 81)

Do you understand how self-justification puts us under the law? (p 81)

Is there a lift in the spirit when self-justifying? (p 81)

Do you agree that we are not suited for self-justification? (p 81)

Father, I do not want to heed the temptation toward the mode of lifestyle that drew me in the past. I see that with Your life in me, I am no longer suited for these things. Thank You that I do not have to work to get rid of them, but I can simply continue to recognize that they are not good for me or helpful for my new Life in You. As I invite out the things that no longer make sense, I look forward to Your freeing me with Your truth.

Chapter 4
The Disciple and God

So often God is portrayed (sometimes even by Christians!) as a very terrible Being who constantly holds us to a standard we can never keep, like some kind of sadistic master. When we buy into this mentality, there is no wonder we want to run away from God! When we relearn who He is, with His incredible love and concern for us, things must change. Realizing the depths of a relationship with Jesus allows us to move forward in truth versus continuing to live as though the lies about Him are true.

The Disciple and God

Are you familiar with your emotional concept of God? (p 83)

Is there a discernible connection between the emotional concept and your childhood authority figure? (p 83)

If Jesus is the only way God is known and revealed, does it stand to reason that the only way you will know God is through getting to know Jesus? (p 84)

Have theology and the laws of God made you run from Him? (p 84, 85)

Have you seen Jesus reveal the love of God so that you draw near to Him instead of running away? (p 85)

Would you say it was important to allow Jesus' light to remove your faulty definitions of truth? (p 85)

Have you wanted the end result immediately while you sit idly by, rather than walking in the Way to the Truth? (p 85)

How does your faulty heart dictionary misinterpret things without the Way that leads you to the Truth? (p 85, 86)

In your broken condition how has life taught you who the Master is? (p 87)

How does the fact that God likes you (even with all that is wrong with you) change your life? (p 87, 88)

Ministering to Desire

What impact is made on you from considering how God ministers to your heart's desire rather than to behavior? (p 88)

Has your behavior caused you to weep? Are you assured this is because the desire of your heart is for Him? (p 89)

To whom in your life do you need to respond based on their heart condition instead of their behavior? (p 89, 90)

Do you see the difference in interpreting Matthew 7:16 with a distinction between fruit and sin? (p 90)

Have there been times in your life when God has proven that His love and acceptance were not based on your behavior but on who you are in Him? (p 92, 93)

Pushed God Too Far

Do you agree that sorrow over failure is proof of being born again, showing the believer has fallen but not fallen away? (p 93)

Have you lived in self-righteousness? (p 94)

How have you allowed lying emotions to dictate your life? (p 95)

Have you established that the way out of unbelief is faith? (p 95)

Can you give examples of times when you have chosen not to believe what you feel or how you behave, and instead believed Jesus? (pp 95, 96)

Will you accept that God's purpose in pointing out sin and failure is leading you to life? (p 96)

A Wiped Memory!

Have you focused your life on a failure when God is not remembering it? (p 97, 98)

How has that failure affected your relationship with God? (p 98)

Are you willing to stop the lying emotions keeping you from His presence and to embrace the truth of who He is? (p 98)

The Disciple and Failure

Have you heard people indicate that if a person fails he does not love the Lord? (p 99)

If believers who fail are excluded from fellowship as being false, then what is the point of the majority of Scripture's calling failing believers back? (p 99)

Have you tried to make the strength of your will be the foundation of your relationship with Christ? (p 99, 100)

Can you accept that God causes no one to sin and that if you do any good, it is actually His doing it through you? (p 100)

What have you heard credited for victory? (p 101)

Do you consider victory a gift, because the ability to walk away from failure rests in the grace and glory of Christ, not in anything a believer can do on his own? (p 101)

Explain how a person chooses to find life in the body or in the spirit. (p 101)

Have you focused on a sin in trying to get past it, only to find yourself more a slave to it? (p 102, 103)

Are you willing to believe that in Christ there is no condemnation, not because you feel it is true but because He has said it is true? (p 103)

Do you understand that sin is not the issue but reveals the issue, which is all that is a hindrance to the expression of His life in us and to our relationship with Him? (p 104)

Can you choose to believe that God can cause your failure to be riches to others? (p 104)

Have you made your failure a ten when it is not a ten to God? (p 104, 105)

What is life teaching you? Could you have learned these things any other way than through failure? (p 105)

What things has God revealed to you as His tens? (p 105-107)

Unlike knowledge from reading or memorization, have you seen that what you learn through failure cuts deeply, leaving scars as reminders of what was revealed? (p 107)

Are you willing to focus on Him, allowing all else to fall into place? (p 108)

The Disciple and the Law of Liberty

Does the illustration of the relationship between parents and children help your understanding of the law of liberty? (p 108)

How life-changing is the revelation that you are accepted with no strings attached because you are His child? (p 109)

Does it make sense that living like a person judged by the law of liberty allows you to show mercy to others as well? (p 109)

Have you abused God's liberty and mercy or seen others who have? (p 110)

How have others tried to put you back under the law? (p 110)

Do you sense freedom from comparisons as you recognize your relationship with the Lord is based entirely in His work? (p 110)

Do you feel drawn to the afflicted and brokenhearted, hoping they might find His liberty as well? (p 111)

Remember, It's a Relationship

What difference does it make to recognize Christianity as a relationship, with all doing growing out of connection and association with Christ? (p 111)

How does your life change when you obey out of love instead of duty? (p 112)

Have you heard people promote perseverance for the reward of heaven rather than for the relationship enjoyed with God? (p 113)

The Divine Escalator

Why do we leave God's presence, where we are more than conquerors? (pp 113, 114)

How different is the idea of the divine escalator from that of overcoming perceived obstacles between you and God on your own? (pp 113, 114)

Do you believe that no one is too far fallen for the divine escalator? (p 115)

Stressed by God

Have you been a "stressed grape"? (p 115)

As you are being stressed, can you remember God is watching over you with special attention? (p 115)

There is No God in the Past

Have you chosen to live in the past? (p 116)

Have you considered how opting to live in the past is choosing darkness that excludes God? (p 116)

If the past created your problems, why would you want to go back and live there again? (p 116)

Will you choose to concentrate on today? (p 117)

Is it a sound argument to say past behaviors and experiences are keeping you away from a God who lives in the present? (p 117)

Have you allowed the enemy to steal the present by moving you to the past? (p 117)

Prayer

Do you see the power of the phrase "the blood of Jesus"? (p 118)

Do you expect great things when asking in the blood of Jesus? (p 118)

The Hurting Father

What is the difference between religion and relationship? (p 119)

What might be the value in sending a child away to get to the end of his rope and find relationship? (pp 119, 120)

God is Love

Do you agree that where love is needed, God must be brought into the equation? (pp 120, 121)

Have you experienced a lift in your spirit when just talking about Jesus? (p 121)

Are you willing to bring the living Christ into a conflict? (p 121)

His Perfect Will

What is God's plan for you? (p 121)

Do you believe it really does not matter where you move or what vocation you have, because God is able to use every event of life to complete His plan? (p 122)

Can you give illustrations of God's guiding every problem that arose from your decisions, with the result that you experienced the expression of His life within you? (p 122)

Have you gotten stuck obsessing on whether you married the right person or if you are in the right job? (p 122)

Can you view misery differently, as indicating there are problems to be revealed and dealt with rather than that the will of God was missed? (pp 122, 123)

Have you believed you are not spiritual enough to hear God and so will never know His will? (p 123)

Can you remember times when God seemed silent either
because you were already in the will of the Father or you had
not done the last thing you heard from Him? (p 123)

What is Not the Will of God

Have you gotten stuck looking for red lights instead of living
freely in the Kingdom of God? (pp 124, 125)

Are you settled with God's habit of alerting us to the red
lights, so we can get on with abundant living without being
sidetracked by constant examination of what is permissible?
(p 124)

How would your life be different after realizing you are
hindered very little by God's red lights? (pp 124, 125)

Is it clear how God's focus mostly concerns our attitude of
avoiding self-centeredness? (p 125)

Have you made the permissible will of God appear difficult
in order to avoid focusing on the known will of God you are
disobeying in action and attitude? (p 126)

Do you believe that as the Good Shepherd it is God's responsibility to show us if He has other plans and what is of major concern to Him? (p 126)

Learning Obedience

How have you listened to guilt and obsession with consequences as presented by the enemy? (pp 126, 127)

As confession brings the focus off of self and on to Jesus, is it clear Satan uses it to ensure that self is still the focus? (pp 127, 128)

If God's desired result of your failure is a simple recognition of your weakness and humility, why are you still stuck focusing on consequences, fear, self-hatred, or years of punishment? (p 128)

Have you grown sick of self through experience? (pp 128, 129)

How have you learned and been cleansed in ways nothing short of failure could have achieved? (p 129)

Are you willing to get up and accept forgiveness and cleansing? (p 129)

Hearing God

Have you taken time to learn how to discern His voice from the myriad of others? (p 130)

Have you tried focusing on the voice of God to you, however you experience it? (pp 130, 131)

Are you willing to tune your ear to the Father's voice? (p 131)

Have you avoided faith while seeking a word, voice, or vision? (p 132)

Are you willing to walk whether you hear or not? (p 132)

Pride

Have you experienced or seen disguised pride as depression?
(p 132)

From all the examples given—self-hatred, self-deprecation,
victimization, self defense, jealousy, hating your
unrighteousness, obsessing on failure and rejection, feeling
that you do not deserve anything, expecting the worst,
and being negative—can you list instances when your own
disguised pride manifested in any such ways? (p 133)

He Makes Your World Beautiful

How have you seen Jesus make the world beautiful for you?
(pp 133, 134)

Father, I see Your love for me in so many ways. I want to
recognize this more and more, focusing on the truth of the
incredible love You continue to show me. Thank You that
behavior comes out of heart attitude, so if my heart is turned
to You, I can move forward in confidence. I do not want to
be stuck trying to figure out Your will or obsessing on my sin,
but rather seeing who You really are and the truth of Your
relationship with me. Thank You!

Chapter 5

The Disciple and Faith

Faith as a topic is often quite skewed in the Christian community. Believers are condemned for not having enough of it, while its value is extolled, but generally many of us have a very limited understanding of it. Mike walks us through various aspects of faith in this chapter, allowing us to comprehend faith in a simple and profound way.

Faith Introduction

Have you ever looked into the eyes of those resigned to hopelessness? (p 135)

Have you been hopeless? (pp 135, 136)

How does a Christian move from hopelessness to hope? (p 136)

Does it make sense that everyone goes away from Christ sadly because they are moving away from hope, and thus from joy? (p 136)

Have you been led to view unbelief as weakness rather than worldliness, self-righteousness, and pride? (p 136)

Have you stood firm in your belief in Christ even when there was absolutely no possibility of your prayer's being answered? (p 138)

Are you one of the "others" who have trusted God for, and yet not received, a restored relationship, the health of a child, a godly home, the salvation of a relative, or just the simple stirring of God within that brings assurance? (p 139)

Do you see how pleased He is with your faith as one of these "others"? (p 139)

Are you willing simply to choose to fix your eyes on Jesus to achieve faith, since wrong focus is the cause of unbelief? (p 140)

Does it make sense that our very being works best in faith? (p 140)

Have you seen faith as one explosion after another as God does everything possible to get us to drink living water? (p 141)

How have you attempted to escape the big ship in which you trust by jumping into a smaller boat? (p 141)

Are you willing to stay where you are, trust God, and cut the ropes to all the smaller boats so you will not be tempted to look at them again? (p 141)

The Disciple Needs Faith

Do you agree that we need to be delivered from our daily hell as well as eternal hell? (p 142)

Have you experienced New Testament salvation, or freedom from daily hell? (p 143)

Do you see that if we believe, we will be saved from our daily hell, and if we are unbelieving, we will be condemned to our daily miserable experience? (p 143)

Why Do You Not Believe?

Can you imagine how it was for God to wake up in a human baby's body? (p 144)

How does Christ's life in you, the life that trusted God and in emptiness conquered all, speak to your condition? (p 144)

What twofold reality is celebrated during communion? (p 145)

Why are you hopeless and unbelieving? (p 145)

Do you understand that you are not being asked to trust in yourself, pull yourself up by your bootstraps and do better, or climb out of the buried coffin on the strength of what you can learn, but rather to trust in a life now living in you that has overcome all you will encounter? (p 145)

Jesus is Faith

Are you willing to deny the flesh and talk about Jesus, allowing your faith to be awakened? (p 145)

Exercising Faith

When have you chosen to speak truth even when you did not yet believe it or experience it? (p 146)

Can you believe you are more than a conqueror, He is your life, you need not look further for God, you are not suited for sin, love is the easy way, you are in the perfect place, and you have married the perfect person? (p 147)

Do you anticipate that as you believe, the Spirit will give you even more faith? (p 147)

Bring Faith to the Table

Describe how unbelief is promoted through the following notions: understanding is the key to living, or following methods and formulas brings success. (p 148)

As you meet others, do you bring faith in God or unbelief? (p 148)

Can you agree all other failures merely emanate from lack of focus on Jesus? (p 148)

What is one way to tell what is most important in your Christian life? (p 148)

Have you experienced the enemy's full resistance when you are trying to focus on and consider Jesus? (p 148)

What experience can revolutionize lives and empower us to love and obey? (p 149)

Faith and Repentance

Have you been stuck wanting a full examination of the filth instead of allowing repentance to flush away the failures? (pp 149, 150)

As we walk in His light and cleansing after repentance, is there any doubt that Christ grants freedom to move on? (p 150)

How have you experienced failures generally arising in areas you consider yourself strong rather than in your weak points? (p 150)

Faith is Finding

Have you wrongly defined finding as getting immediate results or gaining physical, relational, or emotional comfort instead of faith? (pp 150, 151)

Have you wrongly looked around for ease and comfort as proof of God's will? (p 152)

Faith is Being Honest with God

Does it shore up faith to say, "I cannot, but God, You can"?
(p 153)

Are you willing to accept that faith is letting God fix you even
in the face of your deficiencies? (p 153)

Faith and Others

Have you allowed the behavior of a child, co-worker, parent,
or mate to destroy your faith and trust? (p 153)

Do you concur that in contrast people are moved into the
Spirit? (pp 153, 154)

Have you experienced a contrast drawing you out of the flesh?
(p 154)

Faith and Waiting

How does the illustration of "waiting" in the making of rope help you identify your own need for waiting? (p 155)

Have you experienced more joy from waiting than actual possessing? (p 155)

How has the principle of God's fullness of time been made evident in your life? (p 156)

What are you waiting for in faith? (p 156)

Faith and the Glory of God

In what things are you tempted to give God a little push instead of waiting on His action? (p 156)

Have you fought for legalism and taken the glory for the spiritual things done in your life? (p 157)

Have you learned to boast in the Father for His many gifts? (pp 157, 158)

Faith is Upsetting

Have you seen other believers stunt someone's walk in faith by acting according to their own limited faith? (p 158)

How have you experienced God's giving a desire before providing the way to fulfill the desire, so you must step out in faith? (p 158)

Has God given you a desire but you got stuck asking how instead of reaching out in faith? (p 159)

Can you think of times when someone's faith upset you or your faith has upset someone else? (p 160)

Do you see that a relaxed life is one lived in faith? (p 160)

Does it make sense that sin feels wrong because it is against our natures, which are created and held together by Christ? (p 161)

Can you think of some grace teachings you have made into law? (p 161, 162)

Have you experienced the stopping of fleshly behaviors naturally as opposed to your trying to stop them in your own strength? (pp 162, 163)

The Faith Theft

What "bricks" has Satan used to steal your focus from Christ? (p 163)

Have you heard the idea that the way to fight Satan is to keep focusing on him and quoting Scripture to him? (p 163)

Can you identify a focus on Satan as the fighting of a battle already won, and instead simply move focus back to Jesus? (pp 163, 164)

Faith Trusts God for the Family

Are you willing to ask, "Do I have a God?" and then be anxious for nothing (including what your family needs), recognizing that He will be God in your life? (p 164)

Faith Lets God Carry the Burdens

Have you tried casting your burden on another person instead of on God? Can this result in anything but bringing temporary relief and wiping out the person on whom you unloaded the burden? (pp 164, 165)

When you assist others, can you determine ultimately to direct them to turn their eyes to and place their burdens on the Lord? (p 165)

Faith is not Immediate Results

Have you fallen into wanting immediate results instead of realizing that the greatness of your faith is not judged by how much you have received but rather how long you can wait and receive nothing? (p 165)

Have you experienced exhaustion resulting from the attempt to control every area of your life and play God? (p 166)

How does it free you knowing God does not give answers to every situation, but rather reveals attitudes for every situation? (p 166)

Have you realized you may not be free from day-to-day ups and downs, even while maintaining the attitudes God has revealed for the situation, but you should still stand firm to see the fulfillment of the promises in God's time? (p 166)

Can you identify times you have been drowning in all of the information about what to do instead of seeing that Scripture is more concerned with basic attitudes to have? (p 167)

Have you been more focused on doing and immediate results than on believing? (p 168)

How have you tried, covertly or overtly, to change those around you, thinking it will bring instant comfort, rather than waiting to see God work? (p 168)

Faith and Problems

Have you made the mistake of thinking that being a child of God means financial wellbeing, good health, and respect from fellow man? (p 169)

Do you see the trade-off in possessing a life void of material and physical struggle, when it can give rise to pride, violence, hardheartedness, iniquity, an evil mind that knows no limits, malice, arrogance, oppression, boasting, and a disrespectful big mouth? (pp 169, 170)

Would you choose the prosperous unbeliever's life over the suffering believer's life? (p 170)

Is it fair to say the things of God, the ways of God, the desires of God, the life of the believer, and those things given to the believer by God make no sense until we are in the midst of God? (p 171)

When faced with the comparison of the easy life of an unbeliever to your own, are you willing to turn to Him for the life you are living to become special? (p 172)

Have you allowed your happiness and joy to be tied to circumstance? (pp 172, 173)

Would you agree the solution is not to fix the circumstance but to draw near to Him and share in His life as more than a conqueror? (p 173)

Since there is nothing the presence of Christ cannot cure, are you encouraged to look to Him always for a life fulfilled in the Spirit? (p 173)

How has the enemy used guilt to make you run from God and the perceived coming judgment? (pp 173, 174)

Faith and Simplicity

Have you allowed the pursuit of knowledge to help you avoid action rather than accepting the Christian life as simple? (pp 174, 175)

Do you value the importance of not making understanding the end of discipleship, but rather a starting point to bring people to faith? (p 175)

Are you willing to live as a sparrow, realizing you are suited for such a life? (p 175)

The Faith Cycle

In the face of new revelations of self-centeredness, have you heeded the voice of the enemy bringing regret, depression, frustration, and an introspection that makes you more carnal? (p 176)

Have you tried to clean yourself up in order for you and others to feel better? (p 177)

Are you ready to recognize that though you cannot fix yourself, the Lord can, and move another thread deeper into His life? (p 177)

Can you relate to the analogy of the screw's deepening as a picture of our lifelong process of growth in Christ? Are you currently going a notch deeper? (p 177)

Faith Counts

Have you recognized this: If what is promoted as important to life in Christ cannot be accomplished by a person who is only a head, then it is not simple enough to apply to anyone else? (pp 178, 179)

Because faith is greater than doing and is within the grasp of the weakest, does this make God-pleasing readily available to you, even in your perceived strong points? (p 179)

Satan

How have you allowed Satan to become your focus? (p 180)

Can you understand how wrong and dangerous it is to teach that Christians can be possessed by demons? (p 181)

If abiding in Christ keeps a believer from sin, why not begin with abiding rather than obsessing on casting out demons? (p 182)

Does it make sense to examine the source of our emotions, experiences, and what we see in order to determine if it arises from the deceiver? (p 182)

Do you see the problem with claiming demon possession through lineage? (p 183)

Are you willing to recognize Satan's work but camp at the work of Jesus that made him fall from heaven? (p 184)

Father, I do not want anything or anyone to have my focus but You. I realize that when my focus is elsewhere, everything goes wrong and I lose my peace. Thank You for giving me faith and allowing me to cry out that I believe but need help with my unbelief. I see how You continue to provide for me and allow me to walk in faith, even through the hard things. Thanks for making me more than a conqueror in Your Life.

Chapter 6
Discipleship Basics

Unfortunately, in the Christian world we have really messed up a lot of what God originally intended for us. We try to perform for acceptance, we build kingdoms to try to keep ourselves safe, and obsess on everything done wrong—by ourselves or someone else--in an attempt to improve on our flesh. This is all wrong! I think we know it, too, since it makes us sink lower and lower into frustration and failure. In Christ we are able to walk forward, not linger behind in regret or run ahead trying to control the future. Instead, we focus on Jesus, and Jesus alone. He is the only One who will walk through this entire life with us, giving us His Life and showing us victory in Him.

Discipleship Basics

Do you spend a lot of time obsessing on what is wrong with yourself rather than focusing on Christ? (p 185)

Does your definition of a normal Christian life match God's? (p 185)

Discipling on the Fringe

What spokes have drawn your attention away from the hub of Jesus? (p 185)

Have you been convinced you need other experiences to make you whole and support life in Him? (pp 185, 186)

What has been the registration fee required to move you back to the center? (p 186)

Do you see how death is a prelude to life and removes the unnecessary junk hindering a focus on Christ? (p 187)

Are you willing to know Jesus in the midst of the flood that has swept away all that was held dear? (pp 187, 188)

Beginning at the End!

Do you recognize you are complete in Christ and need to add nothing? (p 188)

Have you experienced pyramid preaching? (p 189)

Are you one of the lowliest of believers, a new convert, someone who has never had an emotional experience, or one who has trusted God for something and was disappointed? Can you stand in the confidence that you are complete in Christ and no one has anything you need, because you have everything in Him? (p 189)

What is the difference between miracles trying to build faith and those as a result of faith? (p 189)

Will you choose to believe you are complete in Christ and in Him you are always better off than you felt or thought you were? (p 190)

The Disciple and Sin

Does it make sense to consider that unbelievers will go to hell because of pride rather than sin? (pp 190, 191)

In what ways have you reversed the order of God's priorities, which are pride first, unbelief second, and sin third? (p 191)

Have you recognized that to continue to wallow in guilt and shame is simply pride that keeps you from asking for His forgiveness, as though God expected better from you? (p 191)

Avoiding Self-righteousness and Unrighteousness

Have you been or known someone to be in the Down-and-Out category? (pp 192-195)

Have you been or known someone to be in the Up-and-Out category? (pp 195-197)

Have you experienced or seen a marriage to an Up and Outer? (p 196)

Rather than simply trying to break out of one or the other category, are you willing to make a complete shift by recognizing you are grafted into the tree of Life? (p 197)

The Disciple and Intelligence

Have you come to appreciate the fact that systematic theology is the exercise by which unbelieving believers avoid faith through analyzing, asking questions, and attempting to know God's every move? (pp 197, 198)

Do you understand the difference between trying to dissect God versus having a real relationship with Him? (p 198)

Do you sometimes have or hear criticism of the simplicity and straightforward nature of the Christian life? (p 198)

Do you believe that anyone who has Christ is deep? (p 199)

Is there any better way to an intelligent, abundant life than through a relationship with Christ? (p 199)

The Blown-up Bridge

What other bridges have you tried to build to Jesus? (p 200)

What have you done when God has blown up your bridge? (p 200)

Have you made the mistake of believing you were acceptable to God only as long as your behavior met a certain standard? (p 200)

Is it clear that our access to God is only through faith in the bridge that is Christ and no other? (p 201)

The Law

Have you tried to walk with God through great personal strength and struggle; determination of mind, will and emotion; and the channeling of all talent and ability, without realizing that God walks with us by His own effort and none of our efforts? (p 201)

Are you hiding because trying to observe the Law has made you feel unfit for Him to walk with you? (p 201)

Do you have a list of "to do's," hoping it will qualify you to walk with Him? (p 201)

Do you see the difference between your trying to keep the Law to make yourself worthy of walking with God and His walking with you to make you holy, righteous, and free? (p 201)

Why have you not been able to live a heavenly life on earth? (p 202)

Have you tried to possess through the work of the Law what God gives to man only by way of the work of faith? (p 202)

Is the problem that you do not know, work, or desire enough, or is it that you do not believe that Jesus' walking with you will improve you? (p 203)

Are you improving in order to gain the Son, or is the Son your greatest gain and the One Who will improve you? (p 203)

Have you heard the statement that a believer is a miserable sinner going to heaven? (p 203)

Does it make sense that saying a believer is in a state of depravity is unscriptural, unbelieving, and self-justifying, because Scripture makes it very clear that the condition of the believer is not depravity? (p 203)

Have you received teaching about the depravity of the believer simultaneously with hearing of all the "how to's" of the Christian life? (p 204)

Have you ever found happiness while immersed in examining the flesh of man and the thousands of combinations and manifestations it is capable of presenting? (p 204)

Are you willing to make Christ your focus? (p 204)

Have you tried making Christ the goal instead of understanding, conflict resolution, anxiety reduction, the improved behavior of a loved one, or release from a vexing sin? (p 205)

Do you agree that, at best, earthly discipleship, with its emphasis on flesh, merely creates someone "well adjusted" without Christ, which is not a true improvement? (p 205)

Have you seen Scripture memory emphasized instead of Christ? (p 205)

Why is it that often the disciple who claims to know much experiences very little victory over insignificant events of life? (p 206)

How much does the Kingdom of God within you influence your thoughts and work out its principles in you? (p 206)

Since the command to love our enemies is not given for the sake of adversaries but for us, do you appreciate the deathblow it gives to self and the opportunity to be fed at the feet of Jesus? (p 207)

How have you seen that by loving, you control enemies and are free? Or conversely, how when you tried to mete out revenge have you either become like the enemies or become in bondage to them like their slaves? (p 207)

Is the source of your passion for God earthly or heavenly? (p 208)

Do you believe that the foremost activity of faith lies in your actively waiting on God rather than in efforts to keep the Law? (p 209)

The Disciple and Individuality

Have you become an echo? (p 209)

Are you willing to be a voice communicating Christ's life within instead of an echo? (p 210)

What is the only way to be a voice, to pull away from the herd, to stop pretending, and to live life in its fullness? (p 210)

The Disciple and Miracles

Have you been taught that God's stamp of approval is His supernatural response to our daily activities? (p 210)

Have you wrongly believed that those God loves He blesses and those He wants to get even with find evil? (p 211)

If maintaining this kind of thinking is anti-God, Taoism, and eating from the tree of the knowledge of good and evil, can you accept that God's primary concern is not our comfort or what makes us feel good? (p 211)

How is God using the natural in your life to perfect the answer to your expressed desires, often using pain and suffering to do so? (p 212)

Does it put a lot in perspective to contemplate how all of the natural that comes to us by way of mind, emotion, and body is intended to produce within us the supernatural? (p 212)

How have you seen God bring what is supernatural out of you and your circumstances once the natural drove you into His presence? (p 213)

Have you settled in your heart that all passes through His hands, so you can rest, trust, and get on with life in Him? (p 213)

Does negativity suit a believer? (p 213)

Do you know an occurrence's purpose from observing its beginning? (p 214)

Do the failures of others indicate that life is judging them? (p 214)

What miracles have you experienced as Mike describes them? (pp 215, 216)

Are you willing to see that every day is a significant miracle in Him, something unique to every believer, for the natural makes us supernatural? (pp 215, 216)

The Disciple and a Normal Conversion

Did you come to Christ through an explosion or through a slow and methodical understanding? (p 216)

Have you been led to feel that the explosion is more desirable in the Christian community? (p 216)

Do you see that if you did not have the explosion, you are in the majority and should not wait for one but press on in Him? (p 216)

The Disciple and Vocation

Have you been given guilt trips about missions and evangelism? (p 217)

Have you come to see ministry as living in Him and His living through us, filling all of life's activities with Himself? (p 217)

Have you succumbed to the teaching that spirituality equals activity? (p 218)

Are you willing to stop pressing people for salvation decisions and begin looking for ways to love? (p 218)

Bad Luck

Have you believed that a mental handicap or job loss is bad? (p 219)

Have you felt you have been cursed because of the bad things in your life, due to comparisons with others who seem to have only good? (p 219)

How do you define success? (p 220)

Are you willing to define success in view of the relationship being built with the Lord through what is perceived in your limited outlook to be good and bad, rather than allowing others to define success? (p 220)

The Division of Soul and Spirit

Have you interpreted the quality of life in the spirit by what is happening in the soul? (p 220)

How have you tried to find life in the spirit through the soul? (p 220)

Have you seen God separate soul and spirit in your life? How did He do it? (p 221)

Have you learned that nothing outside the spirit can ultimately destroy you, and thus discovered your freedom? (p 221)

Since adverse circumstances are helping you discover the treasure chest residing in your spirit, can you look at them differently? (p 222)

Weary of the Do-Do's

Do you trust the work of Christ, or do you still trust your abilities to add to it? (p 222)

Do you work in order to be pleasing rather than working because you are pleasing? (p 222)

When you approach Scripture with the mentality that you must earn God's acceptance by doing good, do you recognize that all you will see are the do's? (pp 222, 223)

Have you experienced God's giving you so much to do that you become discouraged and are forced to return to Him via the doing of the Son? (p 223)

Give to No Man/Give to Every Man

How have you tried to milk out of others what you think you need? (p 224)

Has God allowed everything apart from Him to fail you?
(p 224)

Once you no longer look to others for meeting your needs, you are to go back to others; can you envision why you will then seek nothing for yourself and be free from the effects of their rejection? (p 224)

Have you seen believers in the church attempting to give to others without first recognizing that apart from Him they can do nothing? (p 224)

Self-Hatred

Are your actions predetermined by others so that you are not living life but merely responding to it? (p 225)

What spiritual desires do you look for others to meet instead of relying only on God to meet them? (p 225)

Have you experienced self-hatred for needing others' love and acceptance before being able to get on with life? (p 225)

What or whom have you made into a god in your life? (p 226)

Where will you go to find life and the filling of your deepest longings? (p 226)

Can you appreciate the difference between God's making oak believers rather than mushroom believers? (p 227)

How much different would your caring for others be if you did not need them for supplying life to you? (p 227)

Obsessions

What has the enemy used as your obsession to the point that you believed there was nothing else to do in life until it was resolved? (p 228)

Do you recognize your lack of control and that regret is not for believers? (p 228)

Are you willing to give up your obsession and focus instead on Christ? (p 228)

He is Everywhere

What has creation taught you about Jesus? (p 229)

With Him or in Him

Have you believed in spending a certain time with the Lord, and therefore have confined His presence to a time and a place? (p 230)

Do you agree with the greater accuracy of the description about spending time **in** the Lord as opposed to spending time **with** the Lord? (p 230)

Independence

What person or group have you been dependent on to find some of your identity in or against them? (p 231)

Have you seen someone obsessed with an abuse or
maltreatment in their past? (p 232)

In what way could obsession with a hurt cause more trouble
than the hurt itself? (p 232)

Why must we serve something in life? (p 232)

Comfortable with Honesty

When your flesh is revealed through squeezing by others, do
you focus on the ones who squeezed you or your own carnal
response? (p 233)

Have you presented yourself in honesty before God, no better or worse and without justification? (p 234)

Have you experienced a transition in your marriage (or any relationship) from being loving and kind to being carnal and negative? (p 235)

Are you willing to stop destroying, stop excusing, and admit your true condition, in order to find the rivers of living water flowing out of your innermost being? (p 235)

Satisfaction

Have you compared what others have built and placed on a high hill to your own lowly state, wishing you could move inside the manmade kingdom and stay safe inside its walls? (p 236)

How have you attempted to fill spiritual emptiness with activities of the body or soul? Why will that not work? (pp 237, 238)

Have you heard that right relationships are a cure-all,
providing security, happiness, blessings from a pleased
God, and kind conversations? Or that in marriage the right
relationship would produce sexual satisfaction, romance, and
total commitment? (p 238)

In view of what normal relationships actually bring, can you
enjoy your relationships without requiring from them what
they cannot give? (pp 238, 239)

Have you noticed when the spirit is satisfied, the fullness of
body and soul immediately follows? (p 239)

Are you willing to try Mike's exercise of reading Psalm 139
when you are distraught over the future? (p 239)

Total Commitment

Have you experienced lack of total commitment to you during
times of distress or depression? (p 240)

Have you walked on the illegitimate side of wanting total
commitment by expecting others to serve and comfort you in
whatever ails you? (p 240)

Have you neglected efforts toward receiving His daily presence and activity in your life, so it seems abiding in Christ only worked for a little while? (p 241)

Do you spend the day looking for events that prove your feelings of depression, worthlessness, and all the rest? (p 241)

Does it make sense that the more you look to others to act on your behalf, the more closely you will examine yourself to try to find what is wrong? (p 241)

How have lying emotions controlled you? (p 241)

What part did spiritual laziness play in your lying emotions? (p 241)

Do you see that being totally committed is only possible if you have found the One who is totally committed to you? (p 242)

Spiritual Bullies

What kind of bullies have you encountered? (pp 243, 244)

Will you refuse to let the bully define what is weak, strong, intellectual, or religious so that he no longer has power over you? (p 244)

Will you also refuse to measure up to the standard set by the carnal or to play the bully's games? (p 244)

How does taking the road of humility allow the spiritual person to win while losing the bully's game? (pp 244, 245)

Remember the Basics

Are you feeling defeated and as if life is not working? (p 245)

Are you willing to return to the basics and take up the cross of Christ, acknowledging that any death you receive is deserved? (pp 245, 246)

Have you felt that abiding in Christ sounds great but does not work for you? (p 246)

Will you receive by faith and walk in the truth rather than believing truth to be like a panacea that need be received only once and then enjoyed for a lifetime? (p 246)

Have you seen this process (rebel, become angry, justify the anger) in your life when you decide not to walk in truth? (p 247)

If you choose to walk in truth rather than make excuses for why you cannot, does it stand to reason that the power of truth will support you? (p 247)

Are you tempted to make a list of all that must change around you before you can walk in truth? (p 247)

Moving On

How has the Lord allowed failure in one area of your life that caused you to trust Him in a new area and hence move ahead? (p 248)

How have you seen times of barrenness make you go to your roots, which are Christ in you? (p 248)

Father, I see that my failure and the bad times in my life are not a punishment or even a judgment against me. Instead, You allow my failures in order to show Your strength through my weakness. Let me boast in my weakness so that You may increase and Your Life can be seen through me. I acknowledge that only in You can I find total commitment and unconditional love. Thank You for allowing me to have an alternative to living according to my lying emotions.

Chapter 7
The Disciple and Suffering

Suffering is a given in this world, and yet Christians often make more of a mess out of trying to explain the suffering. We are constantly told that we are supposed to be learning a lesson or getting stronger or something through the trial we are experiencing at the time. In this chapter Mike tackles the point of suffering and what we are to do about it, allowing us to move away from trying to play God and simply rest.

Have you been confused by the topic of suffering? (p 249)

Have you heard or believed the notion of suffering so God can test us with discouragement, frustration, and impatience? (pp 249, 250)

What questions has suffering brought up in your life? (p 250)

Have you believed that those who are pleasing to God do not suffer, and those who are suffering have done something wrong? (p 251)

Does the Bible teach that only the unrighteous suffer? (p 251)

Do you believe if you do everything just right, memorize Scripture, witness, have a quiet time, act from Scriptural principles, give yourself completely to Him, and abide perfectly that you will never get sick, always be wealthy, have your family kept from death, be safe in your car, and avoid calamity? If so, can you agree you are attempting to live a godly life to manipulate God into maintaining your comfort, and the true focal point of your life is self and comfort? (p 251)

How have you experienced God's bringing life out of suffering, even though it was deliverance for which you had hoped? (p 252)

How has the suffering in your life driven you to God? (p 252)

Have you tried to keep your children (if applicable) or others in your life from experiencing the squeezing of the world that could bring them to Christ? (pp 252, 253)

What is squeezing you right now to release the life of Christ within you? (p 253)

Do you agree that those who are spiritual have had suffering that brought them to that point? (p 253)

"Every occurrence that is generally thought of as bad is a good event for the abiding believer." How might this statement change the way you look at life? (p 253)

Are you willing to believe that the worst the world can throw at you only serves to release more of the victorious life within you? (p 254)

Have you confused two issues, the one of emotional grieving and that of believing and hoping in Christ, assuming they could not exist simultaneously in your heart? (p 254)

Have you ever failed to receive the consequences you deserved for stupidity? Did you recognize this as God's redeeming your suffering? (p 255)

Do you want to accelerate your Christian growth? Are you willing to rest in the midst of suffering, darkness, emotional swings, broken relationships, or unfulfilled dreams? (p 255)

Is it a relief to know the deep Christian life is suited for weak people? (p 255)

Have you tried to rest while playing God and realized you could not because God is always working? (p 256)

In what areas of your life have you assumed the role of God instead of resting? (pp 256, 257)

Father, I do not like suffering very much, but I realize I know You and am thrust into Your presence when I am in the midst of suffering. Thank You for the hard times that come into my life, for I know You are working in them and comforting me through them. Allow me to remember how You hover around each hard thing in my life, so I do not have to play God and forfeit rest in You. I want to rest in You, not necessarily understanding the suffering but trusting You through it.

Chapter 8
The Disciple and the Word

The pressure that many believers place on themselves to know the "Word" is enormous, and often not the life-giving practice they want it to be. This starts from the confusion of who the Word really is. It is not the Bible, which bears witness of the Word but is too often regarded as of equal or higher importance than Jesus. This creates a mess in that understanding, studying, and figuring everything out are once again up to us. No wonder we are frustrated! If instead we **start** with the relationship with Jesus, all the knowledge and beauty that flows out of the Bible is ours for the taking, without all the pressure to get every jot and tittle explained correctly in order **to have** a good relationship with Jesus. It is getting our order right.

No Answer in Scripture

Have you ever been in need, confused, and lacking direction, but you were not able to find the needed comfort in the Bible? (p 259)

Do you have examples of the Bible's having been proclaimed as the cure-all while problems abound and heart condition seems to trump the Bible at every turn? (p 260)

Have you witnessed or experienced people's attempts to deal with the emptiness within in both positive and negative ways? (pp 260, 261)

Why is a person truly incomplete without Christ? (p 261)

What belief about the purpose of our creation has sidetracked you? (p 261)

What impact is made in your life by the understanding that qualities and behaviors are a result rather than the cause of a relationship with Christ? (p 261)

Have you searched the Bible as an "Answer Book"?
(pp 261, 262)

Do you see the difference made by the order, in that only through the relationship with Jesus is the Bible beautiful and full of helpful knowledge, rather than the Bible's being what allows one to have a relationship with Jesus? (pp 261, 262)

Printing Press

Have you ever considered what believers prior to the invention of the printing press did to learn the ways of God? (p 262)

Have there been times when you have been in touch with the Book but out of touch with the Savior? (p 262)

What small miracles do you need today that come only from fellowship with Christ and the release of His life within? (p 263)

How have you seen it proven true that when Christ comes first, the Book exudes life, while when He comes last, the Book is lifeless? (p 263)

The Word Became Flesh

Do you see that if you view the Bible only as Word becoming word, you are not able to go beyond yourself, for you give power to each word only to the extent that you understand its meaning? (pp 263, 264)

How have you seen religion take what is heavenly and turn it into dead form on the earth? (p 264)

Life Witnesses to Jesus

How do you respond to the statement that if truth needs the Bible to prove it, then it really is not truth at all? (p 264)

How has your life witnessed to the truth? (p 265)

Father, I am thankful for the Bible when it is in its proper place; with Christ first, it can exude life. I do not want to try to confine You to words on a page, because You cannot be contained in mere words. Thank You for being the Word become flesh, allowing me to have a relationship with You in a way that surpasses anything for which I could have hoped or dreamt. I love You, Jesus.

Chapter 9
The Disciple and Others

How many times in your life have you thought that if you could just get someone to change, your life would be so much better and less frustrating? Unless we are hermits, we bump up against others throughout our lives, and we are supposed to, for this is one of the ways the world squeezes Christ out of us. We are mocked, cursed, and taken to task for what we believe, and we generally must fight through encountered rejection by others, whether they are friends or not. The beautiful thing is that we are not without hope in this, for we have a God! In each relationship we have with another, we have a God working in each life in His own way.

Witnessing The Absolute Truth

Have you heard questions from unbelievers about how Christians profess to having the only Way and proclaim the exclusiveness of the Deity of Christ? (p 267)

Have you experienced consequences for shrugging off false religions? (p 268)

Would you agree that if there are no consequences from being disobedient to what man calls truth then it is not truth at all? (p 268)

What results have you seen from following the Truth (Christ), and what consequences have you experienced from not following the Truth? (p 268)

Does the illustration of sacrificing your loved one so others could be saved help you understand how insulting it is to God to say there are a thousand ways to find Him? (p 269)

How does God satisfy both His judgment and His love? (p 270)

Do you live with the recognition that His life has done all, can do all, and flows in you as the life of a vine into the branch? (p 270)

Do you see the contrast between Christianity and all other religions? (p 270)

Bless Those Who Curse You

Have you seen believers who seem a drain on the Body of Christ and yet God provides for them? (pp 270, 271)

How has He blessed you when you were out of tune? (p 271)

Are you encouraged when you see His grace toward others in the midst of their shortcomings, as you see His response to you in your failures as well? (p 271)

Invisible Strings

Have you ever had an experience wherein you were simply relating a few events from your life and the one to whom you were speaking filled with anger? Do you understand that your statement has tugged on some invisible heartstrings in the person? (pp 271, 272)

Can you see the wisdom in finding out why there is a reaction rather than a response to something you said? (p 272)

Have you ever tried telling people what you are not saying to clarify what they hear? (p 272)

Ministering With or Ministering To

Do you see the difference between the pyramid scheme and ministering horizontally, fully acknowledging you have nothing to add to what every believer already possesses? (p 273)

Can you identify people in your life to whom you need to be ministering in the horizontal relationship of the Body? (p 273)

Does a sense of relief come when, instead of choosing not to associate with people, you can simply recognize that you cannot yet minster with them? (pp 273, 274)

Have you been able to identify any of your own flesh in those to whom you minister? (p 274)

Faithful Are the Wounds of a Friend

With any of the wounds you have received, have you asked yourself if the wound expels poison and replaces it with life from above or merely points out error to hinder you through guilt and deliver more condemnation? (p 275)

Can you see the benefit in judging between these wounds and giving them only as much weight as they deserve? (p 275)

When the Disciple Is the Enemy

Can you identify times in your life when your response to negative assessment is love, care, forgiveness, and service, and those actions elevate you above even the justifiably critical person? (p 275)

How might you have allowed the assessments of others to create the very behavior in you they condemn? (p 275)

When have you sensed an awareness of exultation, freedom, and encouragement resulting from love's revelation of the true life within you? (p 276)

Whose behavior have you been focused on instead of responding in love and prayer? (p 276)

Standing Alone

Have you found yourself standing alone? (pp 276, 277)

Did you respond to this standing alone by becoming comfortable with your misery or by comforting yourself with thoughts of how the others will be suffering for the pain they caused you? (p 277)

Have you experienced committing your spirit into the hands of the Lord so that the self-centered you breathes its last, because you cannot be in His hands and exist self-centeredly? (pp 277, 278)

What huge benefit can occur from having been left standing alone? (p 278)

Without Conscience

Have you tried to escape God, in the end finding out every fiber of your being is held together by Him and you live in a world that was created for you? (p 278)

Have you found the whole of your being agreeing that there is a God? (p 278)

Do you recognize that sin is not normal for man and we were made for the Kingdom? (p 279)

Have you seen conscience driving man to show goodness to others, help others, sense compassion for others, and treat nature with some respect? (p 279)

What evidence of conscience in our culture or in unbelievers have you witnessed? (p 280)

How have the laws that hinder expression and satisfaction of the flesh been destroyed in your country? Do you see that once these laws are destroyed, the conscience of the social order is also destroyed? (p 280)

Have you witnessed attempts to replace a destroyed conscience with laws ending in failure and frustration? (p 281)

Can you give examples of the assault being made today on the conscience of those of us who live in the West? (p 281)

How have you seen this statement to be true: "Those who kill a specific area of conscience to allow for the fulfillment of their particular fleshly desire will in the end reap destruction from another fleshly characteristic that was not sought"? (pp 281, 282)

Have you found that the satisfaction promised in the flesh is always just around the corner but never here today? (p 282)

What is the positive result of guilt? (p 282)

Have you ever been angry and realized it was because conscience was replaced by anger, which grants freedom needed to follow selfish animal existence and an excuse for rebellion? (p 282)

How have you seen those without conscience trying to appear as though they enjoyed something lofty that others should experience? (pp 282, 283)

Do you see evidence of our society's dying by degrees while educated in ignorance and in what does not work? (p 283)

Do you feel the excitement of living in this time because you have a God? (pp 283, 284)

How else will you find out that your God can protect your family, provide in crisis, work miracles in family members, displace the enemy, and put to shame all worldly wisdom if you are never in need of protection, food, miracles, wisdom, and victory? (p 284)

Have you had the revelation that we have a God, and has this only true God become an actuality in your life? (p 284)

Verbal Beatings

Have you tried to sort out the language of the world and been confused because it is an alien language to a believer? (p 285)

Have you had others think you sounded mad when talking about dealing with those in the world? (p 285)

What do you do differently when responding to the condition instead of the words and messages of the world or carnal believers? (p 285)

Have you sought the cause for a person's behavior rather than responding to the words and behaviors themselves? (p 286)

Get Off the Throne

How have you erred in taking responsibility for others' actions? (pp 286, 287)

Have you learned that to play God without any of His resources is a frustrating role, for you see what you need to do and yet have nothing with which to do it? (p 287)

Have you experienced an increase in anxiety when you were caught up in responsibility for others? (p 287)

Are you willing to step off the throne, relinquishing responsibility for others and resting in Christ? (p 287)

Have you seen prayer allow you to return to the life of a sparrow as it rightfully releases the responsibility to God? (p 287)

Do you understand that the hardest work you as a Christian can do is to trust God for the changes needed in everyone outside of you? (p 287)

Others Need to Change?

Have you pointed out (either overtly or covertly) the irritating behavior in someone else in hopes of seeing change? (p 288)

Has God revealed a problem in someone else, though He did not want you sharing it with the person because it was not on the top of His priority list? (p 288)

Are you willing to wait on God to reveal a problem in another's life and to bring His healing? (pp 288, 289)

Have you wanted others to change for your own comfort, to make your life easier, and to be free from your hassles and struggles? (p 289)

Do you see that the other persons' problems are revealing more about you than about them? (p 289)

Can you agree that contrast, rather than conflict, changes people? (p 289)

What are some examples of how you can use contrast when dealing with someone who is being frustrating? (pp 289, 290)

Are you ready to keep your eyes off the accusations and on the Father, to maintain moment-by-moment abiding, seeing that His might is there to set you free and He is the only one you want to please? (p 290)

Father, in every relationship I have with another person, I pray that You would set me free as I abide in You. I see I do not have to please every person—I do not even have to make sense to every person! I want to keep my eyes on You as You reveal Yourself to whomever You will, all the while allowing my heart to dwell in perfect peace regardless of the people that surround me. Thank you that I am not limited to my own patience or love when it comes to dealing with other people. Instead, I have access to all the patience and love of God, and as I abide in You, I do not have to live in anxiety and frustration.

Chapter 10
The Disciple and Ending Well

Mike Wells used to talk about how he wanted to walk with Jesus in such a way that when he got to heaven, they would just continue to walk together as if nothing had changed. I thought this was such a beautiful picture of how I want my relationship with Jesus to be. I want to know Him, so it is not a big shock or weird transition when I am face-to-face with Him in heaven, but just a glorification of what I already knew. The way we know Jesus is through the world's contrast, through the hard things that drive us to His presence. This chapter discusses some of these and encourages us to keep on knowing Him in the journey, for He is as much there as in the destination.

Have you believed you will someday "arrive" as a Christian? (p 291)

How would you have answered Mike's question, "If you were standing in the garden with Adam before the fall, what would be the difference between the two of you?" (p 291)

Did you think that Adam was better off than you as a Christian? (pp 291, 292)

What have you learned in contrast? Do you see why it is necessary? (pp 292, 293)

How has God used the world, your body, and your circumstances to allow you to see Him in the most desirable light? (pp 292, 293)

Have you discovered you can see God in all the contrasts of the world, Satan, and the flesh? Is this an encouragement as you learn in that contrast? (p 293)

Have you chosen to see Christ in the everyday events of life, viewing those events as actually very significant? (p 293)

What is your place of revelation? (p 294)

Have you noticed that every time something is revealed about your flesh, a fresh revelation of Jesus is coming? (p 294)

Do you agree that the place you are in right now is the perfect place for a revelation of Him? (p 294)

Have you heard or believed this distorted view of rewards in heaven, where the "holier" man gets to bask in luxury while the "not so good" man gets lesser things? (p 294)

What do you think of Mike's belief that in heaven the jewels, crowns, and more all represent the revelation of Jesus? (p 295)

How have you seen God as much in the journey as in the destination? (p 295)

Father, this journey sometimes includes dark roads, and I forget You are teaching me about Your presence in the contrast. In the darkness You show Yourself to be Light. You show me more and more of who You are all along the journey. I know You bring significance to the everyday events of life, and I want to know You in each one. In whatever place I am right now, thank You that You are using it as the perfect place for the revelation of Yourself.